KU-374-958

BE HAPPY,
MAKE MONEY

How To Turn Your Skills, Talents, Hobbies
& Ideas Into Multiple Income Streams

Jackie Headland

First Published In Great Britain 2005
by www.BookShaker.com

© Copyright Jackie Headland

All rights reserved. No part of this publication
may be reproduced, stored in or introduced into
a retrieval system, or transmitted, in any form,
or by any means (electronic, mechanical,
photocopying recording or otherwise) without the
prior written permission of the publisher.

This book is sold subject to the condition that it
shall not, by way of trade or otherwise, be lent,
resold, hired out, or otherwise circulated without
the publishers prior consent in any form of
binding or cover other than that in which it is
published and without a similar condition
including this condition being imposed on the
subsequent purchaser.

Typeset in Trebuchet

CONTENTS

ACKNOWLEDGEMENTS

Thank you to the people who allowed me to interview them about their Multiple Income Streams and to the authors whose books and articles I've read. Thank you to the thousands of delegates and clients who have shared their ideas views and experiences with me when I'm supposed to be helping them. You have all inspired me and generously shared your knowledge and ideas.

Thanks also to my family who has to live with my passion and enthusiasm for writing my books ... sometimes day and night and at weekends too!

FOREWORD

Who hasn't spent many a Sunday morning throwing around various ideas in order to pay off the mortgage, support children through University, or just to find extra cash to pay the ever mounting household bills?

Jackie has written a how to manual supported with a variety of ideas to appeal to a wide audience and she backs them up with intelligent research and sound advice.

We all possess a degree of entrepreneurial talent. It's about finding out what works for you. For some, being employed and selling handmade crafts at weekends is the way forward. Others, like me, run our own businesses and want to increase the amount of passive income we make.

Combining business advice and information with a coaching approach is what makes this book different from other, 'How to Make More Money' books.

I'm sure you'll find it a source of information, inspiration and support.

Tracey Jefferies
Founder of Ladies That Lunch (www.langmansltd.com)

INTRODUCTION

Aldous Huxley wrote, "Suppose it becomes the acknowledged purpose of inventors and engineers to provide ordinary people with the means of doing profitable and intrinsically significant work, of helping men and women to achieve independence from bosses, so that they may become their own employers, or members of a self—governing group working for subsistence and a local market. This would be a more humanly satisfying life for more people, a greater measure of genuine self—governing democracy and a blessed freedom."

Workers aren't revolting in the streets much these days yet we are seeing a quiet revolution going on in cities, towns and villages all over the world. Small scale enterprise is the new, healthy alternative that many are choosing instead of getting a 'real' job.

This revolution is leading 'ordinary' people to discover their own profitable, satisfying and intrinsically significant work. Huxley and Schumacher would be proud of us! Even better, it's a revolution of the human spirit that's available to anyone ready to reclaim their soul and, in so doing; help create the new art form called Multiple Income Streams.

It doesn't matter whether you work for someone else or run your own business, you can still create multiple streams of income. If you're employed then creating multiple income streams means that you can build your own business(es) while keeping your 'real' job. Once you have built your multiple income streams to the level of your salary and beyond you can then decide whether you want to receive both sets of income or if you want to 'retire' and work from home, building your own business instead.

The beauty and wonder of Multiple Income Streams is that they allow you to use all of your gifts and talents, your skills and knowledge so as to boost your financial security, have fun, and lead a more fulfilled life. Additionally, it is useful to have several income streams going, so that if one income stream dries up for a while you still have something else to keep yourself afloat.

I have listed a wide—ranging number of suggestions in this book to help you generate your own ideas for multiple streams of income. Multiple Income

Streams are both numerous and broad in their scope as are the people who can create them. Business men and women employed in the corporate world, business owners, housewives and househusbands, students, home workers, pensioners and unemployed people can all create Multiple Income Streams and the scope is endless.

This is one of the many advantages offered by Multiple Income Streams — they can be developed and used by anyone —truly offering equal opportunity.

In keeping with the 'equal opportunity' feature I have included income generating ideas and suggestions in this booklet that could earn incomes ranging from £10—£1000+ per hour. The choice is yours.

My purpose in writing this book is to inspire you and guide you to create your own multiple streams of income and I wish you every success in finding your path to joyful and blessed financial freedom and an abundant life!

Jackie Headland

WHAT ARE MULTIPLE INCOME STREAMS?

Many Entrepreneurs and SMEs have a single service or product that they provide to their customers. They may sell speech writing, gardening, accountancy, sports equipment, or architectural services. Similarly, those employed by organisations are of the mindset that they should look for new opportunities within their specialised areas of expertise only.

Specialisation offers many advantages; it's easier to market one product or service and build a solid reputation in one profession or field. However, the reality is that true prosperity and security rarely come from our jobs or one area of professional expertise alone but from using all of our gifts and talents fully.

It is very natural for people to seek the security that their professional knowledge and skills provide. For many this area of expertise was developed so that they could get a 'real' job offering the security that their parents wanted them to have when they grew up. They now spend most of their lives doing something they're good at but don't necessarily enjoy or feel passionate about.

Many people grew up in an era when after leaving school or college they joined an organisation with the certainty of a job for life as long as they were reasonably competent, worked hard, and were loyal. They stayed with that company until they retired 40 years later and received their gold watches.

In the modern era of corporate downsizing, restructuring, and rightsizing to improve the bottom line, anyone clinging to the belief that a 'real' job that doesn't inspire or fulfil them is the trade off they must make so as to ensure lifetime security is passé. Richard Bach, author of *Jonathan Livingston Seagull*, cautions us, "Shop for security over happiness and we buy it at that price."

The real tragedy is that many have developed a fixed income mentality and have bought into the mistaken belief that prosperity and security don't come from pursuing all of their passions, talents and gifts. They fail to recognise that the downside of specialisation is that by deriving all of their profit and/or income from a single source they are generally more susceptible to economic fluctuations and are less profitable or secure in the long term.

The whole idea of multiple income streams is a reflection of the fact that people who have any level of self—awareness realise that they have multiple talents. It makes no difference whether you're an employee, unemployed or self—employed, you can create multiple streams of income to enhance your prosperity and security and create a more fulfilling and abundant life.

You can consider all your options perhaps you could...

- write a book
- manage property
- become a public speaker
- be a consultant or coach
- be a tour guide

...the list goes on.

Just as a river has many tributaries and small streams running into it so too should your bank account have a number of income sources feeding it. A river's level would fall considerably and one day disappear completely were it not for these tributaries adding to it along the way. The same is particularly true of your personal wealth. Your revenue and prosperity are like that river; they need to be fed from many sources.

WHY SHOULD YOU HAVE MULTIPLE INCOME STREAMS?

There are numerous reasons for creating multiple income streams. Barbara Winter, author of the book *Making A Living Without A Job*, tells us that, "Following your own calling is the most responsible thing you can do. Staying in a career or with a business providing a product or service that is less than you are fully capable of is an irresponsible choice."

Each of us has been given a multitude of skills, gifts and talents and when we fail to give them space to flourish we do a great disservice to ourselves, we suffer physically, emotionally, mentally and spiritually.

Many of the people I coach and train have all the outer trappings of success — a wonderful career, great salary and perks, exotic holidays etc. — and yet they confess to frequently feeling unfulfilled and dissatisfied. They long for the time when they can leave the ranks of the working wounded and pursue the things they really love.

What a waste of their talents, time and lives! No wonder they end up bored, burnt out, depressed and unfulfilled. They are labouring under a number of commonly held but erroneous beliefs:

Belief #1: *If something is worth doing I should do it perfectly; I should focus on one thing at a time, specialise, find my niche market and stick with it.*

I have yet to find a successful entrepreneur who has only one iron in the fire at a time. The very nature of an entrepreneur demands variety, ongoing challenge and passion in pursuing a multitude of ideas. Entrepreneurs work hard and long, but rarely end up bored, burnt out and depressed. On the contrary, they live lives filled with passion, enthusiasm and fun. Failure and disappointments are taken in their stride; the next six bright ideas are waiting to be brought to fruition.

Belief #2: *I cannot pursue my dreams unless I can live them 24/7.*

Just because you aspire to being a tour guide or writer or artist or image consultant doesn't mean you have to do any of these things all of the time. You can be a tour guide during the summer holidays, write and paint and be an image consultant at the weekends and in the evenings, and still hold down your 'real job'. Okay, so just until you have developed your dreams sufficiently to step into them full time and can dump the 'real job' (if you want to).

Belief #3: *I cannot pursue the things I love because I wouldn't earn a decent living doing them.*

The 'poor, starving artist' picture many hold in their mind's eye but have never validated holds them back. I know many artists, writers and image consultants etc. who are far from poor and starving! Just look at author J.K. Rowling, artist Bonnie Druschel, and my friend Janie Mackintosh, image consultant extraordinaire! Sure they all took time to build their successful businesses, but isn't the same true of successful careers in 'real' jobs?

In many cases you can actually keep your job while developing your other interests and possibilities on the side. Or you can cover you basic expenses with a part—time job and use your freed up time to work on your other, more rewarding, income streams. Some are lucky and have a supportive spouse or rainy day savings to give them the financial cushion they need but there's nothing stopping *anyone* from making money from their passion.

You will enjoy many benefits by creating multiple streams of income, the biggest advantages are:

Happiness and Success: These things come from doing what you love. To many it is a unique idea that they will be paid for doing more of the things they love to do. They expect a lifetime of working to build a 'successful' career in return for a salary and benefits. Herman Cain reminds us, "Success is not the key to happiness. Happiness is the key to success. If you love what you are doing, you will be successful."

Cash Flow: Business is cyclical by nature and the cash flow of one segment of your business may hold steady, while another rises and falls. This provides continuity that is not present in a single source business or salary.

Freedom: You don't need to feel trapped in a job that doesn't fulfil you; your fulfilment comes from pursuing more of your interests and passions. You get to call the shots in your own life.

Security: The Damocles Sword of restructuring, downsizing or rightsizing need never bother you again. You can sleep easier at night knowing that if you were to fall victim to *one* of these initiatives you already have other income streams to keep you afloat.

Robert G. Allen author of *Multiple Streams of Income* and *The One Minute Millionaire* writes, "It's a volatile future. You'd be wise to have multiple streams of income flowing into your life. Prosperous people have always known this. If one stream dries up, they have many more to support them. Ordinary people are much more vulnerable. If they lose one of their streams, it wipes them out. And it takes them years to recover. In the future, people will need a portfolio of income streams — not one or two — but many streams from completely different and diversified sources.

So that if one streams goes, you barely feel the bump. You're stable. You have time to adjust. You're safe."

Creative Energy: When you're doing the things you love and feel passionate about, you create a lot of positive energy in the world. This attracts all kinds of people and opportunities to you that wouldn't otherwise have appeared.

Variety: When you use all of your skills and talents to generate a number of revenue streams then you pursue all your fields of interest. This gives you greater variety in your life.

When you're living with passion everything you do is done well, this isn't just good for you and your self—esteem it's terrific for your clients and customers too. They have someone helping them who is fully present and alive to their needs.

When you first start developing your multiple streams of income you may find you're working harder and dealing with more details, but in the long term, they offer greater peace of mind, security and fulfilment.

THE POWER OF PASSIVE INCOME GENERATORS

Imagine that you've decided to add another stream of income to your life. You could always get another part time job, but you certainly don't want to get stuck on another hamster wheel — where you're swapping time in direct exchange for money. What you really want are the kind of income streams that that continue to provide revenue even when you're not around to 'mind the store'.

Many small business owners tell me that they have not taken a holiday since starting their businesses and that they work hard and put in long hours too. Surely this is not why they went into business for themselves? I believe that hard work should be balanced with time off for fun; that after the early years of establishing and building a business, owners should be able to take a holiday two or three times a year and still have streams of passive income flowing into their bank accounts.

Robert G. Allen talks about residual income (passive income) describing it as a "recurring stream of income that continues to flow whether you're there or not."

Two Types of Income Streams:
Linear and Passive

Are your income streams linear or passive? Your answer to the question, *"How many times do you get paid for every hour you work?"* will tell you which type of income stream you have created.

If you answered, "only once," then your income is linear. Income streams from a salary are linear. You only get paid once for each hour of effort.

Passive income on the other hand requires an initial creative process to set it up, but once the product, programme or service is developed and in place income flows into your bank account without you having to do very much beyond the occasional bit of maintenance work.

By combining technology and multiple income streams you will earn passive revenue (sometimes called residual income). In other words, once you have the systems up and running, they pretty much tick over on their own with minimal input from you. Selling products via your website is one example of a passive revenue stream — which I like to call PIGs (Passive Income Generators).

The real beauty of PIGs is that they move you from being self–employed to a business owner. Richard Kiyosaki, author of the *Rich Dad, Poor Dad* books, differentiates between the self–employed and business owners as follows:

Self–Employed people are those who want to be their own boss and do their own thing, they value their independence above everything else. Kiyosaki states that the biggest weakness of the self–employed is that if they were to leave their business for a year or so there would not be any business left to come back to.

Business Owners on the other hand, own systems and hire smart people to manage these systems. Kiyosaki states that if business owners were to leave their businesses for a year or so they would return to find them more profitable and running well.

I believe that when we combine technology and multiple income streams we become self–employed business owners. We hire smart people who provide the technological know–how and develop systems that will enable us to bring our multiple income streams to the worldwide marketplace 24/7 and with little attention from us, or the technical experts, beyond occasional general maintenance. You maintain your treasured independence yet grow your business even when you're not around.

The rise of e—commerce has provided more credibility to multiple income stream businesses. Most successful websites generate income from more than one product or service. Think of a website as another tool to create multiple income streams that are passive income generators (PIGs). PIGs unleash a steady flow of income for months or even years after you have invested the initial time and effort to get your PIG up and trotting along. You get paid over and over again for the same initial effort. Wouldn't it be nice to be paid hundreds of times for every hour you invest in your income streams?

For example, authors put in hours of hard work writing their books before they earn a single penny. They aren't looking for a salary cheque; they want to receive a royalty cheque every six months. That's the power of PIGs — they keep flowing as regular as clockwork.

Here's another example. I have been told that the inventor of the tiny battery tester on the Duracell battery apparently presented his idea to the big battery companies, and many turned him down. Duracell recognised a brilliant idea when they saw one and agreed to pay just a few pence per battery for his idea. Now he makes millions, because those passive pennies mount up. The initial investment of many hours of time and effort to create the concept, to package it and then to sell it, now generates a swollen stream of passive income for him and his family. And the best part about it — *he doesn't have to be there!* It flows without him.

When you create your multiple streams of income make sure that you have some that provide you with passive income. Then when you're sunbathing in the Bahamas you can relax knowing that your business is continuing to grow and generate profit while you chill out.

JACKIE HEADLAND

HOW TO CREATE MULTIPLE INCOME STREAMS

Once you understand why you need multiple streams of income, the question is, how do you create them? Well the best way to answer this question is to learn from others who have already done so.

I recently interviewed two entrepreneurs, Dr Chris Fenn and John Wemyss, and asked them to describe how they had created their own Multiple Income Streams.

Dr Chris Fenn

Dr Chris Fenn is a trained nutritionist and when she launched her solo career as a nutritional consultant she planned to do one–to–one consulting with individuals. However, she soon realised she could reach more people by running in–company seminars that could be tailored to her clients' particular lifestyles and running lunchtime seminars for employees on healthy lunch options.

The corporate work she undertook enabled her to conduct extensive research and publish two books about nutrition. These helped to establish her reputation in the wider world and created the opportunity to be invited as 'the nutritional expert' on radio and television programmes.

Chris has two other passions — the outdoors and natural and organic foods — these too have been developed into income streams.

A travel magazine gave Chris an assignment to write an article about climbing Mount Kilimanjaro. Chris saw that there was additional fee earning potential in this assignment and borrowed equipment from the BBC and made a radio programme about her climb to the top of Kilimanjaro.

In the summer months she leads walking groups for Lady Trek (now Island Horizons) on the West Coast of Scotland and for Wild Rose Walking Holidays based in Wales.

Chris's nutritionist expertise combined with her passion for mountain climbing and hill walking seemed to naturally lead her to design diets for mountaineering expeditions. Chris designed the diets for the 1993 British team that celebrated the 40th anniversary of Sir Edmund Hilary's climb to the summit of Mount Everest. They commemorated this event by repeating the climb and simultaneously creating another piece of mountaineering history by including in their team the first British woman to climb Mount Everest, Rebecca Stevens.

Chris also works with British adventurer Pen Hadow who made polar history by becoming the first man to walk 478 miles from the northern coast of Canada, across the moving, melting, rugged sea ice of the Arctic Ocean, to the North Geographic Pole, alone, without any outside help. Chris not only created diets for Pen during this record—breaking attempt, but also creates diets for executives that his company, the Polar Travel Company, takes on 'adventures' to the poles.

In addition, Chris created diets for some of the two person transatlantic rowing teams that hit the headlines recently.

The slide shows that Chris created describing her work with the Everest team and Pen Hadow launched her as a sought after motivational speaker.

Being the Chairperson for the Aberdeen chapter of the Slow Food Group allows her to share her passion for natural food and healthy eating with others and to work with food producers to develop healthier products. The Slow Food Group is an international organisation that promotes the purchase of natural and organic foods and the traditional methods of preparing and eating these foods.

Chris also sells natural and organic soaps, shampoos and bath products (produced by Norwich based company Simply Soaps) at local craft fairs and market stalls.

Chris says, "I've always loved to dip in and out of things. Each of these pursuits could sustain me financially, but then I would miss out on the emotional and spiritual rewards that the multiple streams provide. It is when I combine all my interests and passions that my life becomes fun and fulfilling. My diverse pursuits keep me busy, happy and allow me to live my dreams."

John Wemyss

Necessity drove John Wemyss to create his Multiple Income Streams. He took over Anderson Group Information Services Ltd in April 1999 providing IT Consultancy and Communications Brokerage. The company grew from 1999 through 2001 when he created AGIS Telecom Ltd to allow a split between data and telecoms divisions of the business. His main source of income at that time came from a multi—million dollar contract he brokered with a US company providing satellite communications for a fleet of cable laying vessels worldwide.

The events of 9/11 resulted in his US customer's business depleting due to trade embargoes and finally the contract ceased in May 2002. John's backup had been the telecoms industry that also suffered during this period. Cash flow became a concern and capital reserves were becoming exhausted. Alternative means of income had to be found.

John derived additional, minor income from the provision of IT support to local SMEs and he added low cost website design and hosting services to his portfolio of services. This still didn't generate the level of income he required, so he added the sale of information via the Internet. This worked well since the USA is quite responsive to mail blasts that are seen as taking the initiative to make others aware of goods/services that may be of interest. Unfortunately new EU regulations on Spam meant that John could no longer send out e—mails in bulk even if the users have opted—in. This is because UK ISPs have configured their systems to cut off any suspect Spam servers.

John considered applying an exit strategy but found that he was 'too old' to be considered for a 'real' job. He says, "I know this cannot be the case but I issued an awful lot of CVs for very few interviews, and stupidly in the IT and Telecoms field!" Like most entrepreneurial types, John is not easily held down and before long his next big idea for generating additional income appeared.

At the end of 2003 he decided to find another source of income unrelated to the IT or Telecoms industries. He puts his sales and consulting skills to good use and now consults for a kitchen manufacturer. He finds that this is currently producing more income than all of his other streams combined.

John continues to market and grow his IT and Telecoms business as this is his passion, and he is confident that this market will boom again. He says, "What this experience proves to me is that you can't always do what you want or may be good at — sometimes you have to combine your talents and try something off the wall — you may be pleasantly surprised at the results!"

JACKIE HEADLAND

ARE MULTIPLE INCOME STREAMS ONLY FOR THE SELF—EMPLOYED?

Although multiple income stream creation would seem to be easier for the self—employed, there are endless possibilities for those who are retired, at home or who have a 'real' job in the corporate world, as you will learn later in this book. If you are currently employed consider your job as just one of your income streams. As you develop ideas for additional sources of income you will feel less trapped by the job.

Two employed people and one retired person I spoke to during my research shared their additional income stream ideas with me.

Pam Andrews* launched a dinner party catering business with her sister while working full time with a manufacturing company. Her sister runs the day—to—day operations of the catering business while Pam finds new clients in her travels with her day job and oversees the financial and marketing functions of the business.

Trevor Rhys* drives a van for a delivery company and makes large size games for gardens (e.g. chess, snakes and ladders, four in a row etc.) in his spare time. He sells his products via his website and at craft fairs and exhibitions and generates a tidy second income from this venture.

Debbie Grant is a retired school teacher who runs two direct selling businesses from her home that align with her twin passions for fashion and natural health products. She has built a faithful band of customers over the years who provide additional income streams that allow her to indulge her love of travel.

All of these people learned to appreciate the value of the things they could offer to others. Do you find it hard to believe that you have a service or product others would find valuable? The next chapter, *Getting Started With Multiple Income Streams* will help you to overcome this hurdle.

* Pam and Trevor asked that their names be changed, as their employers do not know about their additional ventures. Some companies have policies about second jobs or ventures, so be sure to check your terms of employment before you launch your additional income streams.

GETTING STARTED WITH MULTIPLE INCOME STREAMS

The development of the multiple income stream mindset is part of the evolution of entrepreneurial thinking widely present in the world today. When you're entrepreneurial (whether employed or self–employed) you are constantly scanning for profit making opportunities, for needs that you can fill by doing the things you do really well and enjoy.

Start by looking for ways to complement your existing business or hobby. Do your friends always ask you to help them to decorate their homes? Do people come to you for relationship advice? It means you're good at it! Learn to appreciate the value of what you offer others.

Let's look at a couple of examples.

If you love baking you could:

- Sell cakes and biscuits.

- Write and sell articles, books and tips booklets about baking and baking products.

- Set up an on—line bookstore full of cookery books via an affiliate programme.

- Offer cookery classes at your local college or even at home, and online through your website.

- Sell advertising space on your website or in your newsletter.

- Set up joint ventures between your 'company' and a company offering a complementary product or service for example selling culinary 'gadgets' via your website in return for the company that manufactures them purchasing large quantities of your tips booklets as 'freebies' for their customers.

As a trainer and coach you could:

- Run training seminars.

- Become a motivational speaker.

- Coach individuals and groups.

- Licence your training courses and sell them.

- Publish articles, books and tips booklets.

- Set up an on–line bookstore full of books related to your areas of expertise via an affiliate programme.

- Sell advertising space on your site or in your newsletter.

- Set up joint ventures between your company and a company offering a complementary product or service.

- Offer consultancy or advisory services related to your product or service.

You will notice that neither of these examples looks beyond one aspect of each individual's talents and expertise. The baking expert may also have very good organising skills and the trainer and coach may love to travel, these open up even more potential income streams.

JACKIE HEADLAND

SET ASIDE TIME

The Nobel Prize winning chemist Linus Pauling said, "The best way to have a good idea is to have a lot of ideas."

Even if you are currently employed or have other commitments that demand your time and attention you can begin by making a pact with yourself that you will set aside time daily, if possible, or at regularly scheduled intervals for the purpose of finding ideas that will bring you additional income streams. These can be small ideas that bring in £10 a time or big ideas that net you £10,000.

You needn't complete the plan to bring your ideas to fruition in one session, but use your scheduled time to get your ideas rolling. Do research, make calls, or write letters — anything that advances your goal of generating ideas.

Here are some suggestions for creating ideas:

Barbara Sher, author of *Wishcraft*, suggests throwing an ideas party.You provide the food and drink and invite your friends and colleagues over to come up with as many creative ideas as they can for using your gifts, talents, skills and knowledge. I love this suggestion because I have always found that my friends have bigger and braver ideas for me than I do for myself.

Barbara Winter, author of *Making A Living Without A Job,* advises us to set aside an hour a week to think of ways to earn another £50 — £75 an hour and then come up with an idea for expanding it in a way that will earn another £50 — £75 per hour; or come up with completely different (additional) idea altogether.

Winter tells us that by starting with these small ideas, we will soon get the £10,000 ideas too.

If you're going to try a number of ideas in order to figure out what you want to do, then this regularly scheduled time can be spent designing a variety of projects.

Join or create a Mastermind Group and spend one meeting a month sharing and creating ideas with/for one another.

Put your inner critic in the cupboard under the stairs for an hour or two so that you can be very honest when you ask yourself the following questions:

What do I want my life to look like?

Having a clear picture of your ideal life will help you to choose those things that would compliment and support this lifestyle.

What would I love to be paid to do?

What are the things that you really enjoy doing? These are the activities that never feel like work and that you probably wish you could spend more time doing. In fact you would probably be prepared to do them without any pay or profit. These activities and interests allow you to be fully in the moment, where time seems to stand still, as you become absorbed in them.

The best place to start with this question is to look at your hobbies. These are often the things you *pay* a fairly significant amount of money to be involved in. Why not do a little research and see if you can make a *profit* from these very same things?

What am I good at?

Make a list of *all* your skills and interests. Are you a terrific gardener? Are you a wizard with home decorating? Do your friends come to you with their computer problems? Do you know almost everything there is to know about caravanning? Do you play the mandolin or speak several languages? Do you make a small fortune from investments? Can you teach line dancing, photography or any other topic? Find the things you already have some skill in, and start a list. You will be surprised to discover where your many talents lie.

What are my work skills?

What are your marketable skills and how much are they worth? Can you contract these skills out or offer them on a part—time basis? For example:

- Computer skills: website design, troubleshooting, taking a temp job that requires desktop publishing skills etc.

- Writing skills: write for the local newspaper or community magazine, create flyers for local small business owners, copywriting, editorial services etc.

- Organisational skills: help others to manage their time better, de—clutter their homes or offices, arrange a birthday party etc.

- Management skills: work part—time for a charity or small business, offer consultancy, coaching and/or mentoring services to small business owners. A gentleman I met at a networking event offers his services to several small companies and works one day a week at each company.

Don't be afraid of markets where you may have some skill, but aren't yet an expert at. For example, many adult education classes are given by people who have experience in the field but don't have teaching qualifications. As long as you have the willingness to put time and effort into becoming an expert in the particular area, you will be able to develop the skills and knowledge you need to succeed.

What is there a need for?

Are you always looking for supplies for your hobby, but can't ever seem to find what you need? It's very likely others are having the same difficulty. So create your own small business to meet this need. Perhaps you love to decorate your kiddies' birthday cakes, and your neighbours would rather pick theirs up at the local supermarket but can't stand the small selection. This is a market for which you already have the skills and interest to meet the needs.

- A room you can rent to a student or tourist.
- A large room or outbuilding that can be offered as conference, meeting or training facilities.
- Land that you can offer to local farmers to allow their animals to graze on.
- A spare garage to rent.
- Do you have anything to sell that you don't need or no longer enjoy? For example:
- Antique or unused furniture.
- Books and specialist magazines.
- Equipment and machinery.

Once you answer these questions you will have identified your potential income streams. Jot down all the ideas that appear in response to these questions, then do your research and discover how you can turn them into reality.

Start an 'Ideas Journal' and whenever you have an idea, jot it down, then set aside time each week to fully explore your ideas. As you follow your inspiration, it evolves and you get more and more ideas. The world of extraordinary possibilities opens up to you.

Think of your multiple income streams as if they were a shopping mall:

- What are your Anchor Stores? These are your biggest cash flow generators. (For Dr Chris Fenn these were her nutritional training and consultancy services.)

- What are your little shops? (For Dr Chris Fenn these were, motivational speaking, books, being a hill walking guide and selling organic soaps.)

Play the 'OR/AND Game' — take the raw idea and continue to repackage and develop it. For example, if you write a book you could create a full day seminar based on it. You could produce CDs and Videos based on the seminars and the book, start a subscription ezine, write and sell articles etc.

By doing this you'll identify and build your multiple income streams and profit centres. Barbara Winter says, "Great fortunes and grand achievements have been accomplished by steadfast devotion to creating tiny successes — which ultimately add up to enormous successes. Making this a habit will be the single best thing you can do to guarantee that your ventures will grow."

Don't become impatient if at first you can only come up with £10—£100 ideas. Whatever you do, *do not* start thinking that your time will be better spent if you work on a £1000 project. By devoting regular time to mastering idea generation at the £10—£100 level, you'll find it much easier to leap into higher levels of income.

Once you've come up with a promising idea commit to staying with it until you can evaluate how your idea fits in with your big picture plan.

For example, you could commit to selling £500 of special occasion cakes a week — three cakes a week is goal that can be realised. Or you can commit to remaining with a larger project until you make your first £10,000, which is also a reasonable goal.

Let's say your long—range goal is to have a business providing organised tours for the over 60's. You have managed two travel bureaus, but neither of them were your business. The goal of owning a touring company still seems totally out of reach.

Raising enough money to start a touring company is an overwhelming idea to you. However, baking half—dozen special occasion cakes at £200+ each, and finding someone to buy them, is not so overwhelming. You are also artistic and could put a caricature on the cardboard cake box, with a phone number for party drawings, and there you have it — the seed for a new income stream!

When you start using this technique you may find you have a few time tested ideas for bringing in cash, but you're very insecure about continuing to be able to do so. You will find, however, that setting aside an hour each day is very easy and that once you start the hour usually stretches into two or three, and always produces some results.

Explore all your options and ideas to discover what the next thing is that you could do. Stick with it; remember it takes 28 days for new behaviours and habits to become a natural part of how you operate. And as L'Oreal tells you, "You're worth it!"

Step out of your comfort zone and do something a little risky. Often those things that scare us the most also help us grow and expand our horizons. Examine all those things that inspire you, all your skills, gifts and talents. Ask yourself, "How can I turn these assets into income generating opportunities?" Then develop a plan to build these ideas into multiple income streams.

MAINTAINING FOCUS AND BALANCE

The possibility for establishing multiple streams of income and PIGs are endless, the challenge is to maintain focus and balance while creating and growing your multiple businesses.

The reality, of course, is that whether you're in sales, administration, running a small business or raising a family, you already juggle multiple projects and competing priorities every day. It's just that once you release your entrepreneurial flair and start generating multiple income streams, each project may become a business in its own right.

Scott Allen of About Entrepreneurs Inc. offers these ideas:

Give your ideas a life of their own. Jot down your thoughts and ideas in a file of their own on your computer or in a journal and anytime you have something to add, you've got the right place for it. Sooner or later, your ideas will start to have a life of their own, and you can stop having regrets for all those ideas that never were.

Make a schedule... You'll drive yourself and others crazy if you flit from one project or idea to another. As Stephen Covey of 7 Habits fame tells us, don't prioritise your schedule, schedule your priorities. The only way to ensure that you are focusing on the next most important thing is to put it into your schedule; otherwise you're going to find yourself focusing on the urgent things in your life at the expense of the important ones. If you want focus you have to give yourself time to focus, free from distraction and knowing that it's how you should be spending your time.

...and then break it! Be flexible. Circumstances and priorities change. One of the big advantages that entrepreneurs have over large corporations is that they are flexible, adaptable and agile. Many opportunities that present themselves are time sensitive, and if you're locked into a rigid schedule, you'll miss them. The trick is to recognise the difference between a time—sensitive opportunity and a distraction. Perhaps we need a new serenity prayer for multiple streamers:

"Grant me the serenity to say no to the ideas and activities that are mere distractions, the courage to act on the ones that are truly opportunities, and the wisdom to the know the difference."

Know the difference between maintenance work and growth work. There's no such thing as truly passive income. Most passive income requires some maintenance work. Rental property has to be managed; websites have to be kept up—to—date, etc. Maintenance work has to be done regularly or negative consequences occur. Growth work on the other hand doesn't have anyone waiting on it but you. Make sure you know how much maintenance work your various projects require so you know how much time you have for growth projects.

Work on only one project at a time, and work on it till it's working for you. This one is the unique key to making this paradox work, and the one that most people don't know and don't do. There is absolutely no point in spending a few hours a week on each of several projects keeping them inching forward little by little.

The trick to both finding focus and creating multiple streams of income is to work on one thing at a time, and work on it until it is at the next plateau. If you are starting out on a project, work on it until it takes on a life of its own.

That may mean getting it to the point where you can share it with potential collaborators or customers, or getting it to the point where it can start generating income. Once a project has started earning an income for you, let it work passively while you work on something else.

Think about it — if you're working on four one-week projects, do you want to finish them all simultaneously at the end of four weeks? Of course not! You want to finish one the first week and let it work for you for three weeks, finish another the second week and let it work for you for two weeks, etc. Doing it this way, you get your projects working for you for six extra weeks vs. the other approach. Follow these simple steps, and you'll soon learn how to live the paradox of focusing on multiple streams of income!

One final point: it is important to target your marketing in order to avoid confusion in the marketplace, particularly if your income streams are very diverse. It can sometimes be wise to focus on discussing only one or two products or services with each client, particularly if they would find it difficult to understand your diverse interest and skills set.

Once you have learned how to build your multiple streams of income and PIGs and at the same time maintain focus and balance, you will keep your business on solid ground, your bank account in healthy balance, and your enthusiasm high.

JACKIE HEADLAND

4 COMMON INCOME STREAMS TODAY

Licensing

Please Note: This information, or any part of it, is in no way intended to be legal advice. If you're thinking about licensing your product or service seek qualified legal advice.

If you have copyright or patent rights over a product or service, you may consider entering into a licensing agreement with another business. This would allow the other party to manufacture, market or distribute your product or material, or provide your service to its own customers or staff, in return for a licence fee and whatever other payments you agree. Licensing is an extremely useful commercial tool that can allow your business to expand without a large injection of capital or exposure to unnecessary risk. A successful agreement can help maximise your business's earning potential and penetrate markets where you may lack expertise.

Each license you grant is typically on a non—exclusive and limited basis, allowing you to keep selling the product, material or service over and over again. There may be times when a company or individual will ask you not to sell to a specific competitor of theirs. That will be a business decision you'll need to make. There may be times a company or individual wants unlimited use of your material for one fee ... another business decision for you.

You can award licensing rights to others for any length of time you choose. You may want each licence to last for a year or two or even for a lifetime. Again this is a business decision you must make.

It is impossible to give you hard and fast rules that work in every licensing situation. You would be well advised to get advice to suit your individual circumstance since each deal is just a little different.

Affiliate Marketing Programmes (AMPs)

AMPs are a quick and relatively easy way to start your own online business if you don't have a product of your own to sell. Many AMPs are free and easy to join.

An AMP is basically an agreement you make with a company to sell their products or services for them, primarily by including a link on your website (or your email signature) to a page on the company's website where people can order the products over the Internet. The link often includes special code that uniquely identifies you as the one who referred the customer to their site.

As an affiliate, you join merchants' programmes, and place their advertising or link on your website. When someone clicks on one of those ads/links and fills out a form or buys a product, you get a commission for that referral or sale, depending on that advertiser's payout structure.

From the company's perspective, by partnering with affiliates they are able to drive traffic to their website, increase their sales, generate qualified leads and extend their brand awareness through a low cost marketing strategy.

Companies will pay affiliates a commission for each product that is sold as a result of visitors that are referred through their affiliates' links. Commissions on sales can range anywhere from 5% to 50%.

Affiliating is a win—win situation for both companies and affiliates.

There are essentially three types of AMPs:

1. Pay—Per—Sale programmes, which are also known as Partnership and Percentage Partners programmes pay either a fixed amount or a percentage of sales generated by your links.

2. In Pay—Per—Lead programmes, you earn a set amount whenever your customer fills out a survey or requests a quote or information.

3. Pay—Per—Click affiliate programmes are similar to Pay—Per—Lead except you are paid each time one of your visitors clicks on the link through to that programme's site.

Amazon.com introduced one of the most famous AMPs with the launch of Amazon Associates in July 1996. Amazon currently has about a quarter of a million sites in their affiliate programme. In the case of Amazon, the referral fees work as follows:

Fees are only paid for users who buy books at Amazon during the visit that results after having followed a link from the affiliated site.

The fee is usually 5% of the sales, though it can be more for certain books if the site linked directly to the product page for that book.

Other AMPs are more advanced and pay based on the lifetime value of the referred customer and not just based on his or her initial purchase. These are very valuable PIGs because they pay you a 'residual income', i.e. you refer a customer to a site *ONCE* and earn a commission from *EVERY* purchase they make from that site *FOREVER*!

An example of this kind of AMP is run by my publisher at www.bookshaker.com.

Before joining an AMP do your homework! A good AMP will offer you thorough training in how to work the programme successfully. There is loads of information and help available from experts in this field — find out where they are and learn from them.

Some Myths About AMPs & Internet Marketing

1. AMPs and Internet Marketing Are Easy Money.

Not true! Like anything else in life worth doing there is no quick and easy route to success. While starting an AMP or Internet business can be relatively straightforward and inexpensive it does takes time and effort to build and market these income streams. However once this is done it is easy to maintain your online business.

2. Anyone Can Make Money Using AMPs.

Once again not true. To be a profitable AMP–entrepreneur requires that you do three things:

1. Take the time to learn how to select and market AMPs effectively.

2. Create a viable plan.

3. Take action to execute your plan.

Leave any one of these things out and you will not build a successful AMP.

3. AMPs And Internet Marketing Are Ways To 'Get Rich Quick'.

Unless you have a wealthy relative who will leave you a large inheritance or you win the national lottery there is no other way to 'get rich quick'.

Do not waste your time, effort and money chasing 'get rich quick' schemes. Invest instead on building income streams that provide your customers with what they want and need. This is the way to build enduring income streams that will allow you to create the lifestyle of your dreams.

4. Online Business Is Free.

As my dear old daddy used to tell me, "There's no such thing as a free lunch!"

AMP and Internet driven income streams don't cost a lot but they're certainly not free. Compared to renting a warehouse to store stock or rental for an office, online businesses start up and maintenance costs are very small and even ongoing costs are small, including little beyond your internet connection, your continuing learning about internet marketing and AMPs, and advertising costs.

5. *It's Too Late To Become An Internet Marketer or AMP—Entrepreneur.*

If you're sceptical then you're probably thinking, 'Yes, but isn't it too late to begin creating Internet or AMP income streams? Surely thousands of others have already cornered those markets."

My answer is that it's almost never too late to start *anything*. Think about it. Is it too late for another supermarket, restaurant, bookstore, boutique, florist or coffee shop to be opened? Is there any point in anyone writing another book or song? Would it be foolish to open another leisure centre or gym? Of course not!

As a matter of fact there couldn't be a better time to become an AMP entrepreneur or Internet Marketer.

But don't take my word for it, let's look at some of the published statistics about Internet Marketing.

At the beginning of April 2003 Nua Internet Surveys reported that:

- By 2004, worldwide ecommerce revenues were expected to total US $2.7 trillion.

- 70 percent of companies have experimented with purchasing online, but less than 10 percent of their total spending is currently being channelled via the Internet.

- A recent search of the internet revealed a report by Gartner Inc indicating that worldwide B2B (business—to—business) revenues are expected to pass $8.5 trillion in 2005.

According to a study from Forrester Research: Almost 20 percent of European seniors have Internet access. The latest survey from the company indicates that the number of consumers older than 55 that are online has increased by 50 percent in two and a half years, up from almost 10 million in 2000 to more than 15 million at the end of 2002.

This increase comes mainly from younger seniors, aged between 55 and 64.

Nielsen/NetRatings, the global standard for Internet audience measurement and analysis, splits senior age groups further and reports that senior citizens age 65 and older were the fastest growing age group online, surging 25 percent year over year to 9.6 million Web surfers from home and work in October 2003. Additionally, within the senior citizen age group, Nielsen//NetRatings found that the number of female seniors online jumped 30 percent, while male seniors jumped 20 percent.

Since October 2002, senior citizens online grew from 7.6 million (5.9 percent of the active Internet universe) to 9.6 million surfers aged 65 plus, making up seven percent of the active Internet universe in October 2003. The second fastest growing age group was Internet users 55 64, which jumped 15 percent from 13.6 million to 15.6 million surfers from home and work.

(Jackie says — This sector of the population is on the increase and represents a potentially huge growth market.)

Additional Forrester research accurately predicted that 2003 sales would grow by at least 25% over 2002 and that online sales will stay strong because

6.8 million US households will shop online for the first time in 2003.

(Jackie says — Please note that this is the number of households in the US only; think about the large market available to you via the internet across the rest of the world.)

Online business–to–business transactions (B2B) are also poised to escalate, according to data from Forrester Research. The firm projects that the European Union's (EU) online trade will surge from the 2001 figure of €77 billion to €2.2 trillion in 2006 — increasing from less than 1 percent of total business trade to 22 percent.

"In 2006, Europe's three major markets — the UK, Germany, and France — will transact at least 23 percent of sales online, and their combined trade volumes will represent a whopping 64 percent of the European Union's total online trade," said Forrester Analyst David Metcalfe. "The rapid growth and high volume of Net based trade in France, Germany, and the UK will pressure proximate countries with deep trading relationships — like Belgium, Austria, and Ireland — to accelerate their migration to the Net."

EMarketer's "E—Commerce Trade and B2B Exchanges" report indicated that Internet—based B2B trade would reach nearly $2.4 trillion by 2004.

The B2B e—commerce projection from International Data Corp. (IDC) is more ambitious than eMarketer's. IDC expects the total worldwide value of goods and services purchased by businesses through e—commerce solutions will increase from $282 billion in 2000 to $4.3 trillion by 2005.

Additional studies have revealed that:

- The number of Internet users exceeded 530 million in 2001 and will continue to grow strongly in the next five years.

- By the end of 2005 the number of worldwide Internet users will double to 1.12 BILLION people. That is one humungous marketplace and it's growing daily!

- Personals/Dating Internet businesses became the largest paid content category in 2002 with US $302 million in revenues, up from US $72 million in 2001.

- eCommerce sales in Q1 2003 reached US $24 billion, a 20% jump over Q1 2002 sales of US $20 billion.

Okay, so you've got the picture! There is a huge existing and potential market waiting for *you* to go and tap into it. The reality is that if you or anyone else has a product that is marketable you should start an Internet business ... today!

Join others' AMPs and create AMPs of your own — let others market and sell your products too.

6. *The Talk About Big Money Is All Hype*

Hype? Well there's certainly a lot of hype out there!

However, more of my daddy's wise words come to mind, "There's no smoke without fire." I believe that wherever there's hype, there's usually an element of truth. Your task is to uncover the truth behind any incredible claims. As I said previously, do your homework and dig until you reveal the truth about any claims made. Ask for testimonials and to speak to others who have signed up for AMPs you're interested in joining. Ask lots of questions and don't agree to anything until you're fully satisfied that any claims are accurate and true.

'Big money' is entirely possible ... if you are willing to apply common sense and take the necessary care and action you will find your Internet Marketing and/or AMP rainbow has a nice pot of gold at the end of it.

eBAY Auctions

This section offers a very brief overview about eBay. Follow the advice offered for AMPs and do your homework before you take the plunge into the world of online auctions. There are many bona fide experts offering help and advice, find them and use them.

What Is eBay?

eBay is an online auction site that offers another way for you create income streams. eBay describes itself as, "A community where individuals and merchants have equal opportunity to buy and sell new or used goods at fair prices. The eBay community is made up of a variety of people: individual buyers and sellers, small businesses and even Fortune 100 companies. Large and small, these members come together on eBay to do more than just buy or sell — they have fun, shop around, get to know one another and pitch in to help.

eBay, simply, is the home of a unique online community.

On any given day, there are millions of items across thousands of categories for sale on eBay. eBay enables trade on a local, national and international basis with customised sites in markets around the world. Through an array of services, such as its payment solution provider PayPal, eBay is enabling global e—commerce for an ever growing online community.

In a recent press release eBay revealed that, "Small businesses across dozens of industries — from accountants and jewellers to photographers and restaurant owners — are coming to the eBay marketplace to access the equipment, supplies and resources they need to start, operate and grow their businesses. As a result, business buying on eBay increased to an estimated $2 billion in global gross merchandise sales in 2003, compared to $1 billion in 2002.

In addition, small businesses are selling on eBay in record numbers. In July 2005, there were more than 430,000 sellers on eBay.com selling full—time or part—time, compared to 150,000 reported by eBay previously.

eBay also reported that there were 157.3 million users of their services. eBay offers a fabulous established marketplace for you to tap into.

Types of eBay Auctions

eBay offers the following types of auctions:

1. The Standard Auction

This is a straightforward auction for a single item you have to sell. You can start the bid at any amount or set a reserve price for the minimum bid you will accept should the item sell.

2. The Dutch Auction

You will need 10 positive feedback points to run a dutch auction. Feedback points are gained when you run standard auctions or make purchases.

A dutch auction is ideal when you have a number of identical items to sell. You start by listing a minimum price, or starting bid, and the number of items you have to sell.

A word of caution regarding dutch auctions: All winning bidders pay the same price which is the lowest successful bid.

3. Category Featured Auctions & Featured Auctions

Featured Auctions are best for higher priced items and items offered in a dutch auction. As with a dutch auction, you need 10 positive feedback points to run a featured auction.

By choosing a Featured Auction Listing option, your item appears at the top of the main Listings page (this appears on the menu bar at the top of every page on eBay).

How Safe Is It To Buy And Sell Items On eBay?

The eBay website informs us that. "The community helps ensure that the eBay guidelines are followed by all members. 'Neighborhood watch' groups, ensure that everyone in the community learns and follows the etiquette and guidelines that are so important in any community."

Most purchases on eBay are protected by one of the following protection programmes:

PayPal Buyer Protection

When you pay for a qualified listing with PayPal, this programme provides coverage up to £250.00 at no additional cost. To see if an item is covered, look in the "seller information" section on the listing and confirm the item's eligibility.

Standard Purchase Protection Programme

Most other items are covered up to £120.00 (minus a £15.00 processing fee) under the Standard Purchase Protection Programme.

eBay has created a powerful platform for the sale of goods and services by individuals and businesses and it provides you with another opportunity to tap into a vast pool of customers for minimum cost. eBay is certainly worth a look—see. Just remember that as with all potential opportunities you need to do your homework.

Property & Investments

There have been many books written on the wealth that you can accumulate by creating income streams using Property and Investment opportunities. These are highly specialised areas that I would not attempt to describe. Instead, I list a few of the books/authors who offer advice about these income stream opportunities.

- *The Rich Dad, Poor Dad* series of books by Robert T. Kiyosaki

- *The One Minute Millionaire* by Mark Victor Hansen and Robert G. Allen

- *Multiple Streams of Income* by Robert G. Allen

- *Money Gym* by Nicola Cairncross

A search of the internet will reveal training workshops offered by these and other experts in this field.

Once again *do your homework before signing up* for anything.

JACKIE HEADLAND

200+ IDEAS FOR CREATING MULTIPLE INCOME STREAMS BASED ON YOUR SKILLS & HOBBIES

Organising Skills

1. There are a lot of people who have an issue with clutter and who need someone to sit there with them and help them sort and purge the piles of things they've collected over their lifetime. Some people find that it can be too overwhelming to do this alone. If you can combine this with a little Feng Shui ability, you'd have a very nice income stream

2. Clean out and organise people's garages and attics/lofts, offer to take away their junk and other things they no longer want. If you're good at restoration you can mend and paint some of their 'junk' to resell at boot and garage sales or even on eBay. This

way you're being paid to clean out the junk and paid again when you clean it up and sell it.

3.   If you have talents in interior design, offer to help people who are moving from huge homes to smaller ones to decide what should go with them and what they really want to keep. If you can also help them to make distinctions between valuable antiques and things with solely sentimental value it helps take so much of the emotional stress off of them, and people will pay handsomely for that.

4.   When my dad died we might have been tempted to pay someone to go through his garage and the garden shed and throw out what was obviously junk and set aside anything valuable or seemingly sentimental.

5.   Help people to pack their suitcases to go on holiday or for business travel. Many people take too many clothes when they travel and others haven't a clue how to pack clothes so that they remain crease free at the end

of the journey. If you have talents in the suitcase packing arena you could be on to a winner with this one.

6. Offer a gift buying service to busy executives. At the beginning of each year they provide you with the birthday/anniversary dates and the names/sexes of the folk they want to send cards and gifts to, specify a budget and leave it up to you. You could ask your customers questions to ascertain likes/dislikes etc. of the recipients of their gifts to personalise them further.

7. Offer to help people with their financial chores. For example, balance their cheque books once a month and write their cheques to pay their monthly accounts. Set up a filing system for their monthly bills etc. Set up reminders on their PC for quarterly and annual bills. You can go to their homes/offices for an hour or two a month, or you can ask your clients to drop their paperwork off at your home/office and collect it when you're done.

8.   Write a tips booklet about how to manage your personal finances more effectively and sell copies to banks to issue to their clients. You can arrange to have their logos printed on the booklets for an additional small charge.

Arts And Crafts

9.   Make jewellery. You can sell it at craft fairs, morning markets, to gift stores, via your website on eBay and through direct selling methods. Send emails that include pictures of your work to friends to tell their friends or ask your friends to throw a jewellery party for you to showcase your wares.

10.   For those of you who are big on recycling — recycle your old jewellery (and other people's). Most people that I know have odds and ends of jewellery that they never use, sometimes it is a piece they don't like much, or beads from a broken necklace, a single earring or cuff link etc.

11. Use old magazines to make interesting collages and display them as pavement art with a tip jar in front of you.

12. Use old magazines to cover cheap or old picture frames, add a coat of varnish to seal and then sell the 'new look' frames at a boot sale or morning market.

13. Decorate a piece of second hand furniture with a collage of glossy magazine pictures or sand the item down, paint and decorate it with stamps that you buy at craft shops, then sell it at boot sales or morning markets.

14. Notice all the neglected and worn out, faded and ugly, painted signs for people's homes and home—based businesses. Buy some paints and stencils and offer to repaint their signs.

15. Paint colourful murals on kiddies' playroom or bedroom walls at £100+ per commission (price will depend on the size and complexity of the mural). Buy some well—illustrated children's books with simple,

bright illustrations and make large copies on the wall. Buy some cute stencils and designs to help you.

16. Create things to sell at craft fairs. Your children can get involved in this too; let them make their own crafty things to sell. Make wind chimes using coloured glass, mirrors, semi—precious stones and crystals. Paint rock babies or animals, make candles, needlepoint or cross stitch, papier—mâché, foam monsters on wire leashes, wood projects, calligraphy, knit scarves in the local football/rugby club colours etc. The list of things you can make and sell is endless.

17. Draw caricatures at fairs, exhibitions, in shopping malls and at grown—ups' and children's parties! I read somewhere that if you are good at caricatures, then you can easily finance a trip to Europe, I don't know how true this is. Take a courier flight to your favourite European city and position yourself in one of the touristy hot spots. Beware the street mafia of artists though ... don't sit down on someone else's turf or

you may get beaten up. Chat to the other artists, and find a place where you won't compete with an "established" vendor.

Doll's Houses & Doll's House Furnishings

18. Either design and build your own dolls houses if your woodworking skills are up to scratch or buy them in kit form and build and decorate them for sale at craft fairs, boot sales or garage sales.

19. There are endless opportunities to create furnishings for doll's houses — a huge market in the USA and UK particularly. Use the web to reach all markets.

Wallpaper

20. Go to a wallpaper store, and search the 'remnants' bin for paper with very tiny prints. Sell small pieces to dollhouse decorators. Search "miniature wallpapers" for retail price comparisons. Be careful for join matches where the customer wants more than one piece. Perhaps cut right

across your roll only, exactly on the repeat line. Then sell only large pieces, for more money, of course. Roll the cut wallpaper pieces in the cardboard cores of kitchen paper towels to keep them in good condition.

Fabrics

21. Collect very fine fabrics that drape very well, for the same purpose. Much of the cloth used to decorate doll's houses does not drape, but sticks out. Fine materials are prized by doll's house lovers.

22. Any standard weight fabrics you have in tiny prints or textures may serve for miniature upholstery.

Beads And Bits

23. Be on the lookout for beads and other small bits that can be built into tiny 'accessories' for doll's houses, such as lamp bases, vases, and furniture feet. The standard scale is 1:12, that means that a 1 inch miniature equals 12 inches actual size. A

discarded necklace, or metal washers, etc., could bring you cash when sold one piece at a time.

Miniature Carpets And Rugs

24. Use a fine crochet hook and fine needlepoint or petit point backing, with several ply silk threads or crochet cottons, to make doll's house carpets and rugs.

Miniature Pictures

25. Produce miniature pictures framed or unframed.

26. Cut out small pictures from magazines and frame them.

27. Digital photography should allow you to produce some original stuff if you aren't an artist.

28. If you're an artist you could paint a few miniature pictures at the end of the day, before the left over paints dry on the palette. Such paintings could sell for a few pounds each.

Miniature Crockery

29. Use Fimo (modelling dough that hardens to plastic when heated) to create a variety of teeny dishes, vases, or other decorations.

30. Display dried flowers, grasses and weeds in miniature glazed pots.

Miniature Walls & Flagstones

31. Go to an ornamental stone yard, and pick up all kinds of bits of gorgeous stone. Chips of shale, in particular, would make fine flagstone floors, patios, and paths for miniature houses.

32. Stone walls and foundations are other ideas. Make miniature dry stone walls in various sizes and shapes.

Miniature Miscellany

33. Tiny straw—bales, twig and bamboo furniture, tiny baskets and hats.

34.   You could keep an eye out for miniatures of all kinds and sizes at boot sales, clean them up and resell them at a profit.

35.   Put up small posters in toy stores advertising your doll's house treasure trove and create your own website to market your products. Attend doll or toy fairs or collectables shows with your displays. Set up at a boot sale, flea market or a craft fair, and wow almost everyone who attends.

Art & Antiques 'Experts'

36.   If you live in a large city and know about art history and the local art galleries and museums you would make an interesting art escort. Advertise as an art gallery tour service to organisations with visitors from out of town. It used to be only men who travelled on business, but today there are many women who do so too. This service would be perfect for people in town for just one day and who want to see the highlights. Or it would be useful for partners travelling with their spouses on

business and who are free during the day and concerned about getting around by themselves. Also many single women would like to have someone to escort them to events like gallery openings and art exhibitions.

37.	Restore old art work if your talents lie in this direction.

38.	Open a service like the travelling antique show that examines and tells people what their art and antiques are worth. Many people find old paintings and treasures in granny's attic/loft/garage and have no clue as to the value of these items.

39.	Tie up with an interior decorator and offer advice on the sort of paintings the nouveau riche should hang on the walls of their penthouses to look more riche than nouveau.

40.	Create art gallery walks around your city or cities you love to visit and know well. Go to all the hotel concierge desks, Bed and Breakfast's and tourist information offices and give them a nice brochure about your art walks (you can create these easily on your computer). You can have a museum walk too (for the people looking to buy art and artefacts). You could even negotiate to get a commission on purchases too if you talk to the gallery owners beforehand!

41.   Design a professional—looking brochure describing highlights of art galleries and museums to see in a spare hour or two and take it to hotel concierge desks, Bed and Breakfast's, tourist information offices and local shops to see if they'd want to buy it as a customer service. Leave a space on the back page so they can stamp it with their business name. Include details of how to get to the various sites i.e. buses or trains to catch and where to get on and off, street names and directions for those who would like to walk there, what entrance(s) to use and include where the nearest toilets and coffee shops are.

42.   Design a simple webpage to draw in clients who want to see the art in various cities you know well. Write little booklets

describing tours and put in notes, bookmark sections of books, and sell these booklets via your website to tourists.

43. You could offer to design a tour to order for special requests or create a package that other guides could use and offer these to tour companies for their guides or customers.

44. You could also produce audio versions of your tours that people could listen to as they explore the galleries and museums they visit when on holiday and sell them from your website.

Negotiators

45. If you love negotiation and you are good at it then you could make a very good living accompanying car buyers and working the deal for them. As someone who pays the asking price for a car I would gladly pay someone a couple of hundred pounds to negotiate a couple of thousand pounds off the asking price.

46. Start a business being the middleman for collectors/traders. Often people are wary of sending valuable items for fear they won't see the money. Set up a webpage and/or a P.O. Box and start building referrals and trusted customers.

Have Car Will Travel

Warning: There are lots of laws and regulations regarding taking fare paying passengers. These include insurance requirements, MOT and special licence plates. Please check with your local authority before launching into any people transport venture.

47. Offer transport for senior citizens who no longer drive (and for any other non–drivers). Take elderly, independent ladies and gentlemen to hairdresser and doctor appointments, and to the supermarket etc.

48. Transport groups of people to the local garden centre—particularly those with a tea room or coffee shop where they can sit down and have a 'cuppa' after their plant purchases are completed. Elderly folk in particular would enjoy an outing like this where someone picks them up and drops

them (and their plants etc.) at home afterwards.

49.   Transport groups of people to the theatre or cinema in the evening. Elderly folk in particular do not like driving at night and would welcome someone picking them up and dropping them off at home.

50.   If you're a stay at home mum you can take your baby along for the ride if dad or granny are unavailable to baby—sit.

51.   Apply to become a luxury car deliverer. This is usually a one—day a week job. Look for adverts in local newspapers that advertise for drivers or contact relevant companies direct. (No passengers allowed with this one though.)

52.   Does your car lend itself to the courier business?   Place an advert in your local paper or community magazine letting readers know that you will courier packages in the local area.   Send out flyers to businesses in your area too.

Cameras, Computers & Technology

53. Have you got a digital camera, a scanner, a computer, other technological wonders and technological know—how? Lots of folks have computers but none of the other stuff so there are loads of ways for you to earn an income using your equipment and technological wizardry.

54. Design a web site for individuals, a new business or an existing one that wants to get on line.

55. 'Tune—up' someone's aging computer.

56. 'Clean up' and dispose of/recycle unwanted computers for individuals and businesses.

57. Create personalised email greeting cards/announcements for births, anniversaries, engagements, weddings, religious holidays, etc. Take pictures of your clients with their families or pets and create the card/announcement, save it on

a disk that they purchase. Your customers can then send it via email to all their friends and family etc.

58.   Take a family's important and historic photographs and documents and scan them on to a disk for easy sharing with other family members. Whenever you hear of somebody's house burning down or being broken into, the one thing they mourn most is the loss of the family photos and important documents, which are often irreplaceable. Your service will scan everything into a format that they can keep on disc, in a safety deposit box, or in a safe, or at another family member's home etc., where the images would be safe.

59.   You could add a brief annotation to each picture, or allow the family to add information onto the disk later, like names and dates, relationships, etc. This would be a great way for all branches of a family to get a copy of every historical picture without a lot of expense. Your clients could drop off the box of pictures or albums and pick them up a week later.

60. People are impulse buyers. Take your digital camera and the new Canon Powershot www.powershot.com (or similar product) to a school sporting event, the community fair, school play, ballet or school concert etc. Put up a big sign that tells everyone attending that you are selling pictures of the kids/people in action at that event. The great thing about this printer is that you don't need a computer to run it. Periodically you go back to your car and charge it from your battery. You can walk around with the camera and print on demand. Parents will pay for a shot of their child making a goal, coming first in a race, having their face painted, highland dancing etc. It is a very good idea to advise the school/parents that you will be doing this beforehand with the current concerns for child safety.

61. You could also wander around a tourist attraction with a sign telling people that you will take pictures of them for a fee. This little Powershot printer (www.powershot.com) is relatively new so

still costs a bit but the price will come right down in time.

62.   Scan children's artwork and create a digital disk for parents. These masterpieces deteriorate over time and take up a lot of room if you have more than one child. You could also use them to create email greeting cards.

63.   You can market this service through school newsletters, offer to donate some percentage of profits to the school

64.   Buy this piece of software (or similar): www.frostbow.com/products/collection_m anager.html (it costs around £20). Then approach art and antique dealers and offer to inventory their stuff for them for say £100—£200 per hour or part thereof. They get a very comprehensive inventory for insurance purposes.

65.   Turn people's videotapes into DVDs. All you need is a computer with sufficient ram and a product such as the HP DVD Movie Writer dc3000 or similar (check computer

magazines or websites for recommendations to suit your particular equipment). Many people (particularly the over 60s) have videotapes of their children, birthday parties, weddings etc. You could even work with a wedding photographer to offer this as a service to their clients.

66. If you know a lot about photography and the technology that goes with it today, produce a 'how to' tips booklet and sell it on your website.

Baking & Cookery

Warning: Health and Safety requirements may mean you (and your kitchen) may need to pass certain food hygiene standards before you can serve/cook food for public consumption. Please check with your local authority before selling your culinary delights.

67. Enjoy baking and/or cooking? Then here are a few ideas to help you earn £100+ an hour.

68. Distribute flyers saying that you will cook a fabulous three course Sunday dinner for ten in the customer's own home, for £200+ depending on the menu selected.

69. Make meals using natural or organic foods for people who are too busy to do it themselves and who would welcome a nice nutritious meal that only requires heating at the end of each day. (By the way Personal Chefing is a hot new career path, one that eventually nets you a whole lot more than £100—£200 a session!)

70. Make gourmet meals for slimmers using natural and organic foods and have them delivered to their homes or offices each day or once a week.

71. Make up a variety of menu planners and a database of recipes to convert to a shopping list and copy them onto a CD. Grade recipes according to factors such as ease of use, fat free, suitability for children to help with preparation etc. Sell the CDs from your website.

72. Start your own web based mail order sweetie, biscuit or muffin factory.

73. Make mustard, chutney, pickles or preserves and sell them by mail order or via the web.

74. Those little recipe books from church groups and Parent Teacher Associations often have terrific recipes. Use your favourite recipes, type them up and print them off in booklet form. Sell them to friends and family and ask them to recommend them to their friends too. Advertise them on the notice boards at local community centres, libraries etc.

75. If you have visual flair and love decorating cakes then make wedding cakes and special anniversary cakes. (See the National Bakery School website at www.sbu.ac/nbs for advice.) Advertise locally and set up your own website too.

76. Cater for special parties, weddings or corporate functions.

77. Some days I would be tempted to pay someone £100 to cook dinners I could

freeze and have available to the family when I'm away from home.

78. Make up gourmet and/or slimmer's picnic hampers during the summer months. Use china plates, silverware and elegant glassware. Ask for a refundable deposit to cover the cost of these items. Advertise by creating brightly coloured flyers and distributing them to homes, under wipers on car windscreens at shopping centres, etc. Insert an advert in the community magazine or newsletter, put notices up on community notice boards, in the local newsagents windows etc. Tell your friends and ask them to tell their friends too.

79. Are you a lady or gent who likes to lunch or dine? Approach mystery shopping companies and become a mystery shopper and diner. You'll need to enjoy filling in the detailed reports afterwards though!

Children's & Adults' Parties

80. Design themed kiddies' parties for £100+ a pop, plus cost of supplies, entertainers, etc.

81. Arrange parties for adults including invitations, cakes, catering and entertainment.

82. Paint faces at kiddies' parties.

83. Teach kiddies to juggle and/or do magic tricks.

84. Teach party guests to line dance or salsa.

85. Make up goodie bags for party guests (kids and adults) containing novelty sweets (or chocolates for adults), small gifts, paper hats, and forfeits (something each guest must do) to add fun to the gathering.

86. Design a treasure hunt (at the party giver's home or elsewhere) with cryptic clues for guests to solve in order to find the 'treasure' at the end. You could put the guests into small teams and give them a

Polaroid or Digital camera to take pictures to prove that they found all the clues. Some clues could require guests to be creative, e.g. when you get to X take a picture of the Martian Red Toed Zorg. Give prizes for getting all the clues correct, most creative photograph etc.

Sewing & Handcrafts

87. Sew Spice Angels — little muslin bags full of pot pourri, herbs and spices that people use in pantries and linen cupboards to keep away insects and scent the linen.

88. Don't sew? Make baby blankets by taking two 1—metre—square pieces of fleece in baby colours for each one. Place the 1—metre pieces on top of one another (e.g., pink on top of blue), cut all along their edges all around — 20 centimetres deep every 10 centimetres — and knot the two—colour fringe. You end up with an adorable, reversible, snugly baby blanket with a charming knotted fringe around the edges. Buy some sew—on appliqués for a luxury touch.

89. Make bags for bags — you know, the containers for plastic bags from supermarkets and other shops, that multiply around the house. Use the lovely materials you can purchase at haberdashery departments in the large stores and fabric shops. They come in all sorts of cute patterns from geese to pigs and frogs.

90. Make shopping bags. People are becoming increasingly environmentally conscious and plastic bags offered by supermarkets are an environmental hazard. I recently bought two of these fabric bags when on holiday in Italy and they are very handy. They fold up nice and small and fit in my handbag ready for when the shopping urge hits me! The other advantage fabric bags offer is that they don't split or tear easily.

91. Create children's pillows in the forms of alphabet letters or numbers. Kids would love to have a set of pillows that spell their name and show their ages.

92. Sell all of these items at boot sales, morning markets or on the Internet using eBay or your own website.

Trade Fairs & Exhibitions

93. Many people I have spoken to who have exhibited at Trade Fairs and Exhibitions have told me that setting up their stands is fine because they feel fresh and excited, but taking it down at the end of the show is a different ball game altogether! By then they'll have been on their feet for 8–12 hours a day, sometimes for 3–4 days at a stretch and handling the visitors to their stands. At that point, the idea of taking down the stand, repacking it and loading it in the car/truck is enough to make grown men weep. You could do it for them, for a fee of course!

94. Visit local trade fairs and exhibitions and hand out flyers (large ones on bright paper so they won't get lost among the stand clutter) offering to dismantle and repack stands. Alternatively, visiting the show at noon and handing out business cards or

going along in the closing hours and chatting up the most exhausted—looking exhibitors might get you some takers.

95. Taking down a stand may take about thirty minutes, but more cluttered stands would take longer. Packing up the stand might be one service; loading into car/truck another. Taking any rubbish to the local recycling centre another.

96. Another great job would be 'stand relief'. Work with the stand—owner right from when the booking is made, and learn the product/service on display. Find out from the exhibition or trade fair manager who is exhibiting and then approach these organisations direct.

Actors, Magicians &
Stand Up Comedians

These ideas are for those who have the gift of gab, a great sense of humour, and a love of the spotlight.

97. Become a 'mock' tarot card reader or crystal ball gazer or psychic and hire yourself out for private and corporate parties, exhibitions, conventions etc. People pay a great deal to hire professional readers to do events, but these readers have been trained and have a specialty. Spend some time beforehand finding out about the people attending the event and weave in some of this information in a fun way when 'reading' their cards. To learn how to put on a convincing psychic reading (for those with no mystical talents) then I recommend The Full Facts Book of Cold Reading, by Ian Rowland www.ianrowland.com

98. If you can show up and say that you read shoes or hair scrunchies or pens, and have a selection to choose from (instead of cards have a fishbowl filled with miniature shoes, scrunchies and various types and colours of pens or whatever). Then just go into action giving a mock reading ... the more outlandish the better! After all, you're only entertaining them.

99. If you're in a big city, where trade fairs and exhibitions are held they often hire several kinds of 'entertainment' to scatter around the exhibition hall ... this includes anything from foot and neck massagers to quick sketch artists.

100. Teach basic acting techniques to professional and would—be public speakers (people who aren't trained for acting but are giving presentations).

101. Teach adults to juggle or do magic — they'll love to show off their skills to their family, friends and work colleagues. I have a friend who is a management trainer and she teaches managers to juggle as part of a management development programme she runs, they love it! I have heard of other trainers and public speakers who use magic to emphasise important points and make their presentations memorable.

102. Sing, dance, play your musical instrument or juggle on the corner or outside a shopping mall with a tip jar in front of you.

103. Buy a bit of stage make—up and do children's face painting in a shopping mall (you'd probably need permission from the management) or in conjunction with a store.

104. Become a voiceover artist. These are the people who provide voices for radio ads, corporate videos etc. See the website www.voiceovers.co.uk/new to get an advice guide.

Bookworms

105. Get listed on Amazon.co.uk/.com and BN.Com etc. as a 'reseller' of used books and sell all those books that have been gathering dust on your bookshelves for years; the ones you know you will never look at again in this lifetime.

106. Amazon has set up an online forum where you can sell your used books. Simply search for the book you want to sell and click on the "I have one to sell" icon when the book comes up. I've done this with quite a few books I had gathering dust, and the prices

you get are pretty good. You mail the book directly to the buyer if it is sold. I like sending books that I no longer read (or I never got around to reading!) to someone who will use and enjoy them.

107. Set up Affiliate links with Amazon, www.bookshaker.com and/or any other sites whose products or services align with yours.

108. Find a remainders bookstore, car boot sales and jumble sales etc. and carefully pick the "good" books for next to nothing. As, you're a guru on your kind of books or area of expertise you can be picky, and select the good ones that sell for a decent price used on Amazon, eBay etc. Then you go home and put them up for auction on eBay or resell them through Amazon.

109. Have you got a lifetime's collection of specialist magazines that you never look at and that take up a lot of room in your home? Sell them on e—bay. My daughter and her husband recently relocated and sold a series of his 'trucking' magazines

dating back to the late 1970s. They made enough money to pay for almost all of their relocation costs.

110. Buy good quality second hand children's books and resell them at boot sales and garage sales and on Amazon and eBay.

111. Love books and children? Contact your local library to assist with holiday activities for children and to lead story time sessions.

Teachers, Tutors & Other Experts

112. Read an introduction to tutoring at www.theglassceiling.com/wib2/ww14_tut.htm

113. Become a qualified English Language teacher and get paid to teach English in the foreign countries where you holiday (visit the TEFL website at www.tefl.com to find out more.)

114. How about tutoring in your home? You could tutor on anything you know a lot about, for example you could teach people

to appreciate modern art and make intelligent comments about it.

115. Teach line dancing or salsa dancing or any other kind of dancing to senior citizens. You can hire space at local community centres very reasonably. Some community centres will include your classes in their adult education programmes and do all the advertising for you.

116. People pay money to go to weight programmes too. Sometimes the 'programme' is little more than a weigh—in and discussion, but the support, motivation and gathering of empathetic souls is worth the expenditure.

117. Lead a meditation group, or a book lovers group, poetry writers group or play readers group. The list of groups you can lead is endless.

118. Invite ten neighbours at £10 each, or five at £20 each, to share their best healthcare, cookery, kitchen tricks, tips and advice etc. You provide drinks and nibbles. I have a

friend who is a superb cook and I would willingly pay £10—£20 to get her to show me how to make her boozy choc mint cheesecake. Another friend is a reflexologist who could teach us how to massage our family members' feet and hands.

Tarot Cards & Runes, Witchcraft & Wizardry

119. If you know how to read Tarot cards and Runes you can offer to do so at parties. You get paid by the host(ess) to show up and do readings for however many hours they want. Charge £50+ per hour. To learn how to put on a convincing reading (for those with no mystical talents) then I recommend The Full Facts Book of Cold Reading, by Ian Rowland www.ianrowland.com

120. Make up spell packs and ask your friends to throw a party and sell them there or via your website. Include instructions, oils, candles, ribbons, shells and stones etc. — whatever someone would need to cast the spell you've created.

121. Sell tarot/rune/astrological readings or spells as gifts for people to give to friends or family members. Create beautiful vouchers with mythical and magical decorations that can be redeemed for a reading or a spell. Offer a price range of vouchers for sale.

Writers, Poets & Storytellers

122. Sell audio CDs of your stories or poems at events and shows. Offer to tell one of your stories or recite a poem you have written to the attendees, then sell the others from a table or stand at the back of the room.

123. Set up a stand at local events and write poems for visitors. They give you the subject and you write a poem for them there and then to take home.

124. Make and sell informational or motivational audio products that people can listen to when travelling to work every day — an opportunity for experts.

125. Make CDs of walking tours through your city or other cities that you know well. Much easier to carry around and listen to than a book – and your customers can look around at the places of interest while listening instead of reading the guidebook.

126. Write newsletters for small businesses and one–man band businesses to send to their clients either by post or via the internet. You could write the newsletter then once it's approved by the business owners send it out to their clients. You could also offer to set up and maintain an up to date list of their clients and e–mail the newsletter to them every month (or weekly/fortnightly if your clients wanted a more frequent newsletter.)

127. If you're good at writing and have a historical bent then offer to research and write the histories of individual organisations.

128. Become a published non fiction author. Buy *Get Yourself Published*, by Suzan St Maur www.suzanstmaur.com to learn how to

pitch your idea or visit my publishers and submit your idea here... www.leanmarketingpress.com

129. Become a published fiction author. Visit the Fiction Writer's Connection website www.fictionwriters.com and the Writers Services website www.writersserices.com

130. Become a freelance writer. Buy *The Freelance Writer's Handbook* by Andrew Crofts www.andrewcrofts.com to learn more about freelancing opportunities and how to tap into them.

131. Scrapbooking is becoming big business as people are regaining an interest in keeping personal journals and diaries to leave behind for their children. This offers an idea for an additional income stream in itself, but if you are a writer then you could offer to write and publish the personal life storybooks of grandparents or great grandparents to give as gifts to family members. I wish that I had a record of all the wonderful stories my granny used to

tell me about her fascinating life in the late 19th and early 20th century.

Profit From Clutter

132. Sell your unused and unwanted possessions on eBay (the fees are nominal). You can sell almost anything there — a keyboard, curling tongs, books, videos, CDs, mini trampolines, other exercise equipment, comics, roller blades, new skin care products, clothes, art and antiques ... the list is endless.

133. Get rid of a couple of antiques or pieces of expensive jewellery that you aren't that attached to. Take them to a dealer or even an antiques fair.

134. Have a garage sale or boot sale to get rid of your junk. "One man's junk is another man's treasure."

135. Speaking of which, visit boot sales and garage sales and buy good stuff cheaply, clean it up and resell it at a higher price. I know a couple of people who buy furniture

at garage sales or flea markets, fix/clean them up and resell for 3 or 4 times the purchase price.

136. Organise a community garage sale at a local hall, school or community centre. You can sell your own bric a brac and charge others a small seller's fee to set up their tables and sell their goods.

Health & Beauty

137. Do you have beautiful nails? Paint other people's nails at home (yours or theirs). My elderly and almost blind mum would love to have someone come and give her a 'professional' manicure at home.

138. Give pedicures at home (yours or others).

139. Give massages, reiki, reflexology at lunch times in offices or during the day or early evening in your home or at others' homes.

140. Find small and select manufacturers of natural and/or organic soaps, shampoos, bath salts/oils, cosmetics or household cleaning materials and offer to sell their

products at your local craft fairs, boot sales and market stalls etc. You could even make your own range of these products and become the next Anita Roddick of Body Shop fame!

141. Are you particularly good at a sport like football or martial arts? Run a training academy in the summer holidays and take kids off their parent's hands while sharing your knowledge and keeping them out of trouble.

142. Train to be an image consultant, fitness coach or beautician and charge the fees you deserve.

143. Become a diet guru or slimming consultant. Organisations like Slimming World, Weight Watchers, Rosemary Conley and others all offer licences. You'll need to go through the programme yourself before your can purchase a licence.

144. Become a cosmetics consultant. Organisations like Avon, The Body Shop and Virgin Vie, to mention a few all offer

licences to sell their products. You get a commission based on the sales you make and hefty discounts off the products you purchase too.

Off The Wall & Unusual

145. Become a professional thief: get paid to break into people's houses to discover weaknesses in their security systems. (Arrange this 'break in' with the owners beforehand or you'll get arrested!)

146. Sit as a model for an art class at the local college or university.

147. Start a granny sitting service. Better health care and diet means we are living longer and increasingly grown up children are looking after elderly parents who may or may not live with them. Offer to visit elderly parents when the family is on holiday or away for a weekend. This will provide the parents with company and give the family reassurance that their parents are being checked on while they're away.

148. Offer a Karaoke or DJ service to residents in retirement homes and for silver and golden wedding anniversary celebrations, 50+ birthday bashes etc. You'll need to have all the old favourite tunes from World War 1 & 2 as well as the 1950's, 1960's and 1970's. My mum and her friends at the retirement home love to sing along to all their favourite tunes from their mis spent youth whenever the occasion allows.

149. Become a bouncer at private parties, weddings and other private events. Gatecrashing is on the increase so this could be a growth market.

150. Are you a keen fisherman or bird watcher? Organise trips for different levels of expertise, from novices to experts. Offer taster sessions for people who would like to 'test the water' before buying equipment. You can hire out equipment to them at a reasonable fee, and perhaps even offer a shopping service where you buy their kit for them once they're ready to pursue the particular hobby fully.

Learn From Others

151. Buy books by Mary Hunt and others who teach you how to pinch pennies. With the money you save, you could easily have an extra £100.

152. Find someone who is knowledgeable and can show you how to invest your money and make it grow. There are many professional financial coaches to choose from. Always check with other satisfied customers before selecting the right coach for you.

153. Start up an investment club and charge everyone £10 a time to attend meetings, get a financial expert along to the first couple of meetings to get you all up and running and on track.

Baby Sitting

Warning: Check with your local authority first before offering your services as a baby sitter or child minder in your home or others. There may be strict procedures you need to adhere to.

154. Baby—sitting on New Year's Eve, Burns Night, Christmas Eve etc. when it can be

difficult to find baby sitters. You could keep several children overnight.

155. Baby—sit four children at a time to give groups of stay—at—home mums who are friends a break.

Pets & Pet Fashion

156. If you walk for exercise, offer to walk pedigree dogs at the same time (on the perhaps mistaken assumption that owners of pedigrees will pay more than owners of merely marvellous mutts).

157. Design and manufacture pet fashion accessories such as ear muffs, diamante bows for top knots and tails, bow ties, body warmers and scarves etc.

158. Design and manufacture up market bedding and fashionable clothing for pampered pets. Faux fur, spangles and metallic fabrics, Burberry tartan, Halloween, Christmas and Easter outfits for dogs, cats and even ferrets and rabbits.

159. Manufacture a range of gourmet treats for pampered pets.

160. Manufacture environmentally friendly and organic products for pets and animal and bird residents and visitors to gardens, including all—natural treats for birds, bedding materials for small animals and pet clothing made from hemp fibres

161. Manufacture pet perfumes and bone—shaped mints for sweeter doggie or moggie breath.

162. Manufacture massage and aromatherapy treatments for pampered pets to enjoy the spa treatment.

163. Give reflexology or reiki treatments to stressed out pets.

164. Create and manufacture stylish and safe transportation systems and harnesses for all pet categories including rabbits, hamsters, and birds.

165. Design and manufacture monogrammed clothing, bedding and feeding dishes

166. Design and manufacture edible greeting cards for pets on their birthdays and holidays.

167. Create a range of designer luggage for pampered pets now that those with passports can travel too!

168. Set up a pet grooming service.

169. Set up an in house pet sitting/house watching service for people going on holiday.

Gardens & Gardeners

170. Grow seedlings in pots and sell them at boot sales and morning markets.

171. Grow bean sprouts and sell them at boot sales and morning markets.

172. Grow fresh herbs and sell them to local restaurants and hotels, at boot sales and morning markets.

173. Grow fresh herbs in pots and print and attach food recipes or herbal remedies

using the specific herb and sell these at boot sales and morning markets.

174. You can dry some of your herbs too and sell them as described for fresh herbs.

175. Manufacture your own organic compost and bag and sell it at car boot sales and morning markets, even to garden centres if you can manufacture sufficient quantities. Advertise it in your community newspaper too and offer a local delivery service.

176. Write Tips Booklets offering all your hard won gardening expertise and sell these via your website, advertise them in your community newspaper, and to your friends and tell them to tell their friends about your wonderful booklets too. You could offer general gardening hints and tips or specialist advice, for example Growing Orchids, Creating a Butterfly and Bee Friendly Garden, Creating A Kitchen Windowsill Herb Garden etc.

Research & Typing Services

177. There are lots of different types of people who need internet research done regularly. Design a web site with samples of the types of information you are prepared to research for people or organisations. Include typical prices based on either the time it takes you OR the complexity of the subject to be researched. Some jobs require hourly rates, others can be done for a flat fee, and still others may need a time and materials rate structure.

178. Find people with looming deadlines that need an hour's worth of research or writing or typing pronto!

179. Type up and proof read theses for students from their written notes.

Business & Professional

180. Look for Joint Venture Opportunities. Seek out opportunities to create joint ventures with others. Ask, "How can I help you and

how can we work together to achieve our goals and create multiple income streams?"

181. Write a tips booklet that features hints and tips around your particular area of business and professional expertise. To learn more about creating a tips booklet go to www.TipsBooklets.com.

182. Write a book. Yes, writing a book is a big project, but with "print on demand" publishing you can now print short run books very affordably in a brief period of time. You can also sell them via your website in 'hard' copy or as e—books. An added benefit of writing a book is that the title of "author" is impressive and you will have a marketing tool that will immediately promote your expertise.

183. Write Reports. Do extensive research into areas that are of importance to your existing and potential clients and then sell these special reports.

184. Write Articles. You could also use your research to write articles that you sell to newspapers and magazines.

185. Train to become a life or executive coach. Coaching can be done at anytime and face—to—face or over the phone. It can be fitted around other jobs or interests that you have. There are a large number of Coach Training providers available, it is a good idea to speak to existing coaches and ask them where they trained before committing to a programme.

186. Use your well—developed business plan writing skills to help new business owners produce professional business plans.

GET PAID FOR YOUR EXPERTISE

You don't have to have formal qualifications to be an expert, you just have to have lots of experience.

187. Become an expert witness. Have you published a widely respected book about your area of expertise? You can increase

the odds of becoming an expert witness by listing yourself in the directories that the legal and media communities consult. Take a look at two websites: www.expertwitness.co.uk and www.experts.com

188. Set up an internet service like the one developed by internet researcher Mel White who launched a pay per question service, 5 Minute Mentor www.melwhite.com/5mm.htm with a very simple cost structure and pay system: five dollars for a five to ten minute reply, roughly 2 4 paragraphs. You e mail her your question, she e mails you when she has an answer ready, you pay and then she sends you the answer. Similar sites are answers.google.com and www.keen.com

189. Become a Talking Head. Many experts who appear on TV do so for little or no recompense. But some, designated as "consultant" in their on screen credit line, get paid to be accessible for interviews in their area of expertise. Getting your foot in the door for such opportunities has to do

with making yourself accessible and responding immediately to a call from the media. You should be quick with pithy and provocative comments and be willing to set aside other plans when the network needs you. Give your local radio and TV stations a call and let them know you're available if they need an expert in your field. Even better, send the station boss a copy of your book and let him/her know you're there when they need you.

190. A Script Consultant. Films, TV dramas and feature length documentaries often include a behind the scenes role for content experts who advise on the likelihood of plot lines, the authenticity of props and procedures and factual background in everything from medicine to corporate takeover strategy to furniture. Lots of people would undertake such an assignment for the glamour and ego gratification alone, but you'll be well paid for your contribution. As with becoming a talking head, cooperativeness, accessibility and flexibility matter just as much for

succeeding in this sort of role as does your knowledge. Your work might amount to a concentrated, one time advisory consultation or a long term contribution to an ongoing series. Some useful websites: BBC www.bbc.c.uk/writersroom, Euroscript www.euroscript.co.uk, NATPE www.natpe.org, PACT www.pact.co.uk, and The Screenwriters Workshop www.lsw.org.uk

191. Put together a workshop people actually need. What's the biggest problem your target market faces and what do you know about solving it? This is the key to filling your workshop. Find the problem you are uniquely qualified to solve. Do not rely on vague promises like "improving your life" or "boosting your income". Offer us something we can really use, such as "How to Make More Money and Enjoy Your Life."

Miscellaneous

192. If you live in a tourist area offer to open or close people's holiday homes.

193. Trace someone's family tree and prepare an on line presentation that they can email to all the relations.

194. Tune up or repair a friend's car or major appliance.

195. Restore old photographs and enhance them.

196. If you are artistic you can also turn a photograph into a painting.

197. Clean silver and brass ornaments at boot sales and flea markets.

198. Set up a generator and charge for people to test electrical goods at car boot sales.

199. Make and sell unique, high quality tee shirts or polo neck sweaters. Buy iron—on transfers for laser printers so you can

create your own quotes or pictures to add to make unique garments.

200. Approach pubs, clubs and other 'entertainment and social' organisations, take photo's of their staff and quiz/darts etc. teams and create transfers using these pictures to put on the establishment's tee shirts.

201. Start a playgroup for adults. A group/class doing the kinds of things kids do — so adults can reconnect with the experiences they loved as kids!

202. Some days I would be tempted to pay someone £25 to do:

    a. an hour's worth of ironing, or

    b. an hour's worth of matching up outfits for me to wear the following week.

    c. An hour's worth of cleaning the house, garden etc.

203. Anything that will cause small children to pester their parents is probably a good money—spinner. Make doll's clothes, angel or fairy wings and wands, devil horns and tridents, swords and shields, windmills, soft toys etc. Look at kiddies' current favourite television shows and knit jerseys with the popular characters on the front, use your imagination — again the list is endless.

204. Assemble flat packs of furniture or large items of sports equipment for people who are DIY challenged or who don't have the time to do this themselves.

205. If you've got good DIY or Handy Man skills then offer these services locally. Increasingly, people are too busy with their careers, to have the time or inclination to do small repair jobs themselves.

206. Offer an aquarium set up and cleaning service. Once again many people enjoy having an aquarium but don't have the time to care for it properly.

207. Set up a swimming pool cleaning and maintenance service somewhere hot – like Spain!

208. Set up a window blinds and awnings cleaning and maintenance service.

209. Set up a boat maintenance service. Powerboats require maintenance regularly and in particular when they have had a lengthy 'over winter' break.

210. Set up a house, upholstery and/or carpet cleaning service. Approach the property letting agents in your area and let them know about your services, they use these types of cleaning services regularly. Advertise in local newspapers and magazines too.

211. Collect and dispose of old Christmas trees.

212. Set up a gutter cleaning service or window cleaning service.

213. Write letters for others. Elderly people who are somewhat disabled appreciate this service in particular. Approach local care

homes and sheltered housing complexes and advertise your service on their notice boards.

214. Set up a balloon design and delivery service. Create themed displays for weddings, product launches, parties etc. For example heart shaped balloon decorations for Valentine's day or Wedding parties.

215. Set up novelty bicycle tours in your local area.

216. Buy ethnic jewellery, gifts and novelties when on holiday and resell them at local fairs and boot sales. If you're really adventurous you could import larger quantities of popular items and sell them as above or at parties organised by your friends and your friends' friends or even create your own mail order catalogue (paper based and electronic) to sell products to a wider public.

217. Finding the perfect gift can be an exercise in frustration for many people. If you love

shopping and have a knack for finding unusual items at affordable prices then you can use your skills to create custom made gift baskets for all age groups/tastes. This product would lend itself to direct sales and to home party and internet sales too.

218. Is home décor a talent you possess? Do you always find just the right ornament or picture for every room in your home and as gifts for your friends' homes? Offer your skills to home owners in your local area. Set yourself up as a 'home image consultant'. Create a flyer that you can drop into the letterboxes of new homeowners in your local area offering to provide them with a free consultation and report on how they can create their own elegant style in their homes and gardens. Have a supply of pictures/ornaments etc. that you can use to demonstrate how small touches can create a dramatic transformation. These could become a useful additional income stream when potential clients buy them on impulse.

219. Set up a recycling service. This is another hot area for future business opportunities.

220. Work part time for a charity. Visit www.jobsincharities.co.uk to look for opportunities that appeal to you.

I'm sure that you can come up with hundreds more ideas for your multiple income streams. Many of your ideas, like mine, will require minimal start up costs to begin. What you contribute is your skill, knowledge, experience and enthusiasm.

Don't forget to do your homework before you begin, consider who your customers are and how you can reach them. Also check out your competitors to determine what they offer, their prices or rates and how you can make your product or service unique. Start small and actively gather feedback from your customers. All these activities will create a solid foundation on which you can build your successful streams of income. Finally, be sure to find out about rules and regulations regarding tax, health and safety etc. early on to ensure you're on the right side of the law.

Always remember that your business is more likely to succeed if it is something you love to do and not just a way of making money. I have certainly found that when I pursue those things I'm passionate about, the money always follows.

I hope I have ignited your desire to turn your passions into profitable multiple income streams and wish you every success in your ventures. Have fun and good luck!

JACKIE HEADLAND

ABOUT JACKIE HEADLAND

Jackie Headland is a popular and enthusiastic facilitator, coach, public speaker and author who helps businesses and individuals to shine. Helping people to succeed is her heartfelt passion and she shares simple, practical tools during her training programmes, public seminars and in her books.

Some of Jackie's seminar topics include:

- The Art Of Achieving Success
- The Magic Within
- The Cure For Boredom And An Unfulfilled Life
- Maintaining Your Enthusiasm In Tough Times
- Leading Change
- Strategies For Personal Change
- Maximum Influence
- Essentials Of Negotiation
- Foundations Of Management
- Handling The Differences In Others

- Magnetic Networking Masterclass
- Create Your Perfect Life
- Greatest Year New Pathways
- The Power Of Focus
- Personal Branding and Power Networking Masterclass
- Bluffers Guide To The Impostor Syndrome
- Power Tools For Women, Plugging Into Essential Skills for Work & Life

...and many more

To find out more about how Jackie can help you and your business achieve the levels of success you desire e—mail her at jeheadland@aol.com

Let Bookshaker.com Become One of Your Multiple Income Streams

If you've enjoyed this book please tell your friends, family, colleagues, customers and suppliers about it.

My generous publisher, BOOKSHAKER.COM will reward you handsomely for doing so thereby proving what I told you earlier, that if you sign up to a brilliant affiliate programme everybody wins.

BOOKSHAKER.COM will pay you a healthy 10% commission on sales of all their products just for recommending this book and helping your friends and contacts to get their hands on the simple and useful ideas I have shared with you. And it doesn't end there, visitors you refer are **tracked for 22 years** so even if they don't buy on their first visit, you'll still earn when they come back and buy my book or any other later on.

Find out how easy it is become an affiliate with BOOKSHAKER.COM just visit this link now...
http://www.bookshaker.com/affiliate_info.php

www.BookShaker.com
Your Online Haven of Wealth, Health and Happiness

Ever wondered...

How it would feel to achieve your biggest goals and dreams?
Why some people seem to have it all while others struggle?

Stop wondering and start winning...

Whether you want to improve business, get better
at influencing others, make your fortune or simply
positively transform yourself, you'll quickly find
what you're looking for by authors who write
from experience at www.BookShaker.com

Articles - Tips - Previews - Reviews

Register now at www.BookShaker.com

Plus, if it's your first visit, benefit from a
10% welcome discount when you register

Printed in the United Kingdom
by Lightning Source UK Ltd.
117552UKS00001B/31